D1492035

BRIDGES

HOW THEY WERE BUILT

BRIDGES

J. STEWART MURPHY

Illustrated by

CHARLES KEEPING

London

OXFORD UNIVERSITY PRESS

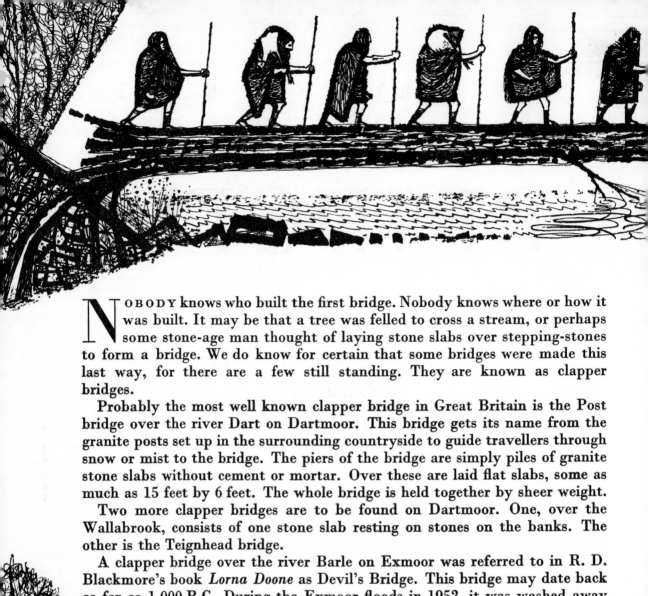

NOBODY knows who built the first bridge. Nobody knows where or how it was built. It may be that a tree was felled to cross a stream, or perhaps some stone-age man thought of laying stone slabs over stepping-stones to form a bridge. We do know for certain that some bridges were made this last way, for there are a few still standing. They are known as clapper bridges.

Probably the most well known clapper bridge in Great Britain is the Post bridge over the river Dart on Dartmoor. This bridge gets its name from the granite posts set up in the surrounding countryside to guide travellers through snow or mist to the bridge. The piers of the bridge are simply piles of granite stone slabs without cement or mortar. Over these are laid flat slabs, some as much as 15 feet by 6 feet. The whole bridge is held together by sheer weight.

Two more clapper bridges are to be found on Dartmoor. One, over the Wallabrook, consists of one stone slab resting on stones on the banks. The other is the Teignhead bridge.

A clapper bridge over the river Barle on Exmoor was referred to in R. D. Blackmore's book *Lorna Doone* as Devil's Bridge. This bridge may date back as far as 1,000 B.C. During the Exmoor floods in 1952, it was washed away by the flood waters. County engineers, using a crane, managed to recover all the stones from the river bed. Some of these stones, weighing 4 or 5 tons, had been washed as much as 100 feet downstream.

Clapper bridges are thought to have existed in Spain, Ancient Egypt, Babylon and China. One such bridge still stands at Fu-Kien in China. This thirteenth-century bridge is called the Lo-yang bridge and has spans of 70 feet.

The first bridge on record was built by Menes, king of Egypt, about 4,600 years ago ; and about 4,000 years ago one was built at Babylon. Many more must have been built but forgotten, their records lost in the distant past.

Many secrets of the strength in bridges lie in the shapes as well as the materials that they are made of. The arch construction gives strength to many

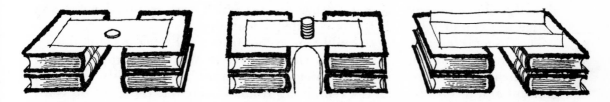

bridges, and there is an experiment, that you can try for yourself, which will prove how strong an arch is. Arrange four books in the way the picture shows. Now lay a sheet of ordinary writing paper across the space between them. You have now made a simple beam or slab bridge like the clapper bridges. Put one penny in the middle of your bridge and it will probably collapse. Now take another sheet of paper and form an arch under your bridge, as the second picture shows you. You will probably find that your arch bridge will hold up five or more pennies. Another way in which strength may be given to a bridge is to build it with two sides to it. You can test this by folding up the edges of your piece of paper as shown in the third picture. This is known as girder construction.

ABOUT 2,000 years before the Roman conquest, arch bridges were being built in the cities between the rivers Tigris and Euphrates. Traces of stone arch bridges have been found in places as far apart as Mexico and China. These arches were very crude and simple. They were built by laying each stone of the arch a little farther out over the river than the one below it.

The Etruscans, in central Italy, were probably the first people to build bridges with the true semi-circular arch that we use nowadays. They built their arches of wedge-shaped stones over a timber frame, which was removed when the bridge was completed. This frame is called a centering.

The Romans learned how to build true arches from the Etruscans and, during their campaigns of conquest, carried the art all over Western Europe, leaving many beautiful bridges, some of which are still standing. Probably the most graceful and beautiful of all the remaining Roman bridges is the Pont du Gard in France. This is an aqueduct or water-carrying bridge and is built in three tiers of graceful, slender arches. The topmost tier, carrying the water channel, is 160 feet above the river Gard, and the whole bridge is about 860 feet long.

Sometimes the Romans decorated the approaches to their bridges with huge triumphal arches. The Pont Flavien at Saint-Chamas in France has a 20-foot high arched entrance at either end.

The first concrete bridge was built by the Romans in the sixth century A.D. at Amalfi. This bridge is still standing. There is little left, however, of the Roman bridges built in Britain. They were probably mostly built of timber and, despite the fact that the Romans had perfected ways of fireproofing timber with alum and protecting it with oil and resin, these bridges have long ago rotted and fallen. During the demolition of the old London bridge in the last century many relics were dredged up, showing that a Roman timber bridge had existed on that site.

6

When the great Roman empire fell, most of the art of bridge building, like so many other arts, was lost and forgotten in the Dark Ages that followed. Many bridges fell because they were neglected and left unrepaired, many more were destroyed in the wars between the barons. Vast areas of countryside were left with no bridges at all, and travellers had to cross rivers by fords or in boats.

Many of the bridges built in the middle ages had pointed arches : these are called ogival arches and were the type used by the Persians in their bridges. It seems that, in many parts of Europe, people had forgotten how to build a true semi-circular arch. However, the true arch did survive in Italy.

One of the first bridges to be built after the fall of the Roman empire was the one named in the well-known French song *Sur Le Pont d'Avignon*. This most beautiful bridge at Avignon was designed by St. Benezet, and building began in 1177. When he died in 1184 the saint's body was laid to rest in the little chapel he had built on the bridge. Three years after his death the bridge was completed.

Many of the bridges built in Europe in the Middle Ages were fortified and could be used as defence posts to prevent an enemy from crossing rivers. One fine example of these war bridges is the Pont Valentré at Cahors in France. This beautiful old bridge is the one pictured on the French 12 franc postage stamp. Built between 1308 and 1355, the Pont Valentré has six pointed arches and is surmounted by three towers, one defensive tower at each end and a central look-out tower.

Two defensive war bridges are to be found in Great Britain, one at Monmouth called the Monnow bridge, the other, Warkworth bridge, in Northumberland.

The widest span of any existing bridge built in Britain during the Middle Ages is to be found in the Twizel bridge over the river Twill in Northumberland. The underside of the arch of this bridge is ribbed, which shows that, even in the Middle Ages, men had learned how to cut down the weight of a structure while still keeping its strength.

7

PROBABLY the most famous of all the arch bridges is the Sydney Harbour bridge in Australia. This bridge, which has a span of 1,650 feet, carries four railway tracks, a roadway 57 feet wide, and two footpaths. The roadway is 172 feet above the water of Sydney Harbour.

The bridge was designed in London by Sir Ralph Freeman; the steel parts were made in Yorkshire and carried to the other side of the world, to Sydney, to be erected. The steel for the arch alone weighs 38,390 tons.

Before the bridge was built, a scale model of it was made and a giant testing machine was designed to put pressures of up to 1,250 tons on the model. It was tested under this machine until its steel parts buckled and rivet heads flew off, and finally the whole model collapsed with a shattering roar.

When the engineers were satisfied with the strength of the model, work started on the bridge itself. Firstly, where the steel ends of the arch were to rest, four great holes were dug, each one 90 feet long, 40 feet wide and between 30 and 40 feet deep. These were dug out of solid rock and then filled with concrete. Steel bearings were set in the concrete. Each of these bearings was designed to take a weight of 119,700 tons.

Behind these foundations, part of each of the great pylons was built. These pylons were made from granite quarried at Moruya, 150 miles south of Sydney. It took 240 men 6 years to quarry enough granite to build the two pylons.

Each half of the steel arch was built out from the shore until the two met in mid-air 800 feet from the shore and 450 feet above the water. To stop the two halves from collapsing while they were being built, they were tied back with steel cables, with their ends buried 100 feet into the rocks below. These cables were $2\frac{3}{4}$ inches thick, and each side was tied back with 128 of them. They had to be strong, because apart from the tremendous weight of the arch, each half was carrying a 600-ton crane which moved out as sections were built on to the ends.

It was a great feat of engineering, for when the two ends were completed, they met and matched exactly. However, the engineers did not have it all their own way, for just before they were joined, a violent gale blew up and the

two ends, with their two great 600-ton cranes, started to swing backwards and forwards past each other. The bridge stood up, though, and the joining was completed.

The cranes now started working backwards, fixing the hangers and the deck underneath the arch. While this was being done, one of the men working on the bridge slipped and fell 172 feet into the water, but he only broke two ribs and was soon back at work on the bridge.

When the bridge was completed, 72 railway engines were driven out on to it to test it. This made a load of 7,600 tons.

The Sydney Harbour bridge was opened on the 19th of March 1932, and had cost £4,218,000 to build.

THE Birchenough bridge, another great arch bridge, was built by British engineers over the Sabi river in Southern Rhodesia. This bridge, which has a span of 1,080 feet, carries a light roadway for two lanes of traffic with a footway suspended underneath.

The most amazing thing about this bridge is the fact that it only cost £134,600. The same steel cables that had been used to hold up the two halves of the Sydney Harbour bridge, while it was being built, were used to hold up the two halves of the Birchenough bridge and, when the arch was completed, they were cut up into lengths and used as hangers for the deck.

This was such a fine, slender bridge, that the effect of winds upon it had to be considered, so the designers built several models of it, and tested them in a wind-tunnel. This was probably the first time that wind-tunnel tests had been used on bridge construction.

The Clifton bridge was built in 1897 across the gorge below Niagara Falls. It was built out from either side of the gorge, each half being tied back to the cliff behind it until the arch was completed. Steel bars were used to tie the two halves back. These bars were removed when the two halves met, leaving the 840 foot arch standing on its own.

This bridge had a very severe test in the winter of 1898. It had been a hard winter, and great quantities of ice formed on Lake Erie above the falls. This ice broke up and came over the falls in huge blocks. Three-quarters of a mile up-river from the bridge, these great blocks jammed from shore to shore forming a giant ice-dam. The water level of the river rose 25 feet behind the ice. Suddenly the ice-dam burst and a great tumbling, roaring mass of ice and water surged down towards the bridge. The ice crashed against the ribs of the bridge: the whole structure shuddered but stood firm, its steel ribs cutting like knives through the ice.

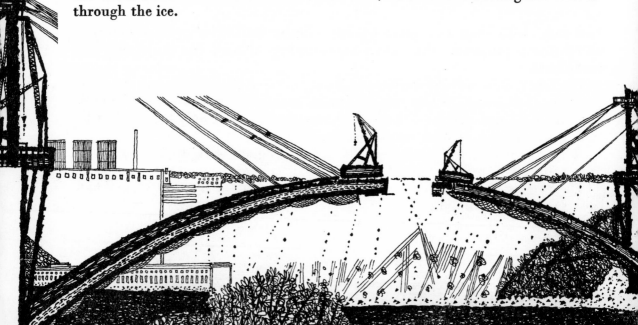

A concrete wall was built to protect the bridge, but in 1938 another ice jam broke the steelwork at the ends of the ribs. Within four years a new bridge of high-tensile steel was built. This bridge, called the Rainbow bridge, has a span of 950 feet. While it was being built, safety nets were slung underneath. These nets saved the lives of four men.

At Victoria Falls the mile-wide Zambezi river drops 400 feet into a gorge, and here, across this great gorge, the Victoria Falls bridge was built. This bridge, like the Sydney Harbour bridge, was designed by Sir Ralph Freeman. It is a flat-topped arch, and had, originally, two railway tracks running over the top of it.

The engineers who built the Victoria Falls bridge were faced with the problem of getting materials for the northern half of the bridge over the river, since it was to be built out from both sides at once. A rocket was fired across the gorge with a fine cord attached to it. A wire cable was attached to the cord and hauled over. To the wire a steel rope was attached; this was hauled over and an engineer crossed on it to supervise the hauling over of a heavy steel cable. This cable was supported on towers and carried an electric trolley designed to carry up to ten tons.

The cable was 400 feet above the river. A huge safety net was slung across the gorge below the place where the bridge was to be built, but the men said that it made them feel nervous, so it was removed.

Gustav Eiffel, the man who designed the famous Eiffel Tower in Paris, also designed some bridges. Two of these were arch bridges. The first, which he designed with T. Seyrig, is the Pia Maria bridge over the Duero river at Oporto in Portugal. The second is the Garabit Viaduct over the Truyère in the south of France. This bridge has a 540 foot span, and carries a single track railway 400 feet high over a deep valley. The Viaur Viaduct is also attributed to Eiffel. This graceful arch, which was built about 1880, has a span of 722 feet. The arch, which rises 380 feet above the river, is hinged at two supports on the sides of the valley and at its centre. Each half was built out from its supporting hinge. This was the first bridge to be built of steel in France.

11

THE UNITED STATES OF AMERICA

NEW YORK BRIDGES ~ *George Washington · Brooklyn · Hell Gate · Williamsburg · Manhatt*

HELL Gate bridge, built over the East river in New York and designed by Gustav Lindenthal, has a span of 977 feet. This bridge presented the engineers with some problems for its foundations had to go down from 37 to 107 feet in order to reach rock strong enough to take the weight of the arch. When the ground had been dug away under water, a split between 15 and 60 feet wide was found in the rock. A concrete arch had to be built over this split in order to form a base for the foundations. All this work was carried out 70 feet below the water level of the river.

When work is carried out under water, it is usually done inside a caisson. This is a large, hollow chamber, which is floated out to a position directly above the point where the foundations are to be dug. It is then weighed down

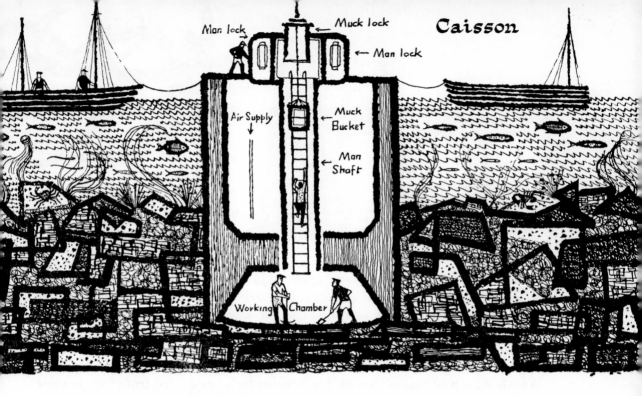

Man lock → Muck lock ← Man lock

Air Supply ↓ | Muck Bucket | Man Shaft

Working Chamber

until it stands with its cutting edge on the river bed. As you will see from the picture of a caisson, there is a working chamber at the bottom. The water is kept out from all the working areas of the caisson by compressed air. The deeper the working chamber has to go below the surface of the water, the higher the pressure inside it has to be. At 120 feet below the surface, the pressure is 52 pounds per square inch. This is the highest pressure at which men can work with safety. Even then they have to be very fit and strong to work under these conditions.

As the men in the working chamber dig out the soil under them, the caisson sinks lower, and this goes on until they reach rock or clay that is hard enough to take the weight of the bridge. The soil and rubble that is dug out is loaded into a muck-bucket and carried up the bucket shaft and out through an air-lock. This allows the bucket out without letting the compressed-air escape.

When the men leave the caisson, they too have to pass through an air-lock. When they do come out, they have to go straight into a re-compression chamber, where the air is pumped up to the same pressure as that of the caisson. The pressure is then allowed to drop slowly to normal air pressure. For men who have been working for 4 hours at 40 pounds pressure, this takes 105 minutes. If the pressure is not brought down slowly, bubbles of nitrogen gas form in the bloodstream of a man, causing terrible pains and sometimes even death. This effect of pressure changes is called the 'bends'. Fortunately it is a rare occurrence nowadays.

13

MANY bridges, designed to span wide rivers or bays without central support, are designed as suspension bridges. As the name suggests, the deck of the bridge is suspended, or hung, from a support above it. Some of the great steel arch bridges are also suspension bridges, for they have the deck suspended below the arch. Two good examples of arch-suspension bridges are the Sydney Harbour and Birchenough bridges.

Another form of suspension bridge has the deck suspended from two or more chains or steel cables. The cables are held up by two towers, one at each end of the space to be bridged, and the cable ends are anchored down into the ground behind the towers. The deck of the bridge is built out from either side, and suspended by steel hangers from the main cables.

One of the first bridges to be built in this way was the bridge over the Menai Straits. It was designed by Thomas Telford to carry the Holyhead road from Wales to the Isle of Anglesey.

Work began on this bridge in 1820 and it was opened in 1826. Two high towers were built with cast iron saddles to carry the sixteen wrought iron chains that were to carry the weight of the deck. Each of these chains was one third of a mile long and weighed 24 tons.

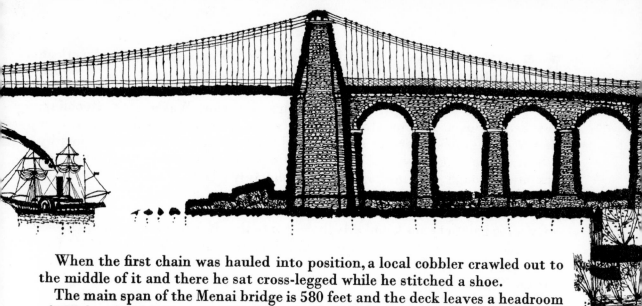

When the first chain was hauled into position, a local cobbler crawled out to the middle of it and there he sat cross-legged while he stitched a shoe.

The main span of the Menai bridge is 580 feet and the deck leaves a headroom of 100 feet for shipping to pass underneath. This deck was made of timber and, unfortunately, was not very strong, for 13 years later it was wrecked and part of it fell into the straits. The mail-coach to London was approaching the bridge at the time, and the bridge keeper, who was unable to cross the bridge to give a warning, rowed across the straits in a small boat, arriving just in time to stop the coach from galloping on to the wrecked bridge. After this the deck was rebuilt in heavier timber. In 1893 a new steel deck was built, which lasted until 1940, when the bridge was reconstructed. This was done in two and a half years, without the bridge having to be closed to traffic. The sixteen wrought iron chains were replaced by four high-tensile steel ones, weighing 1,300 tons. The deck was completely rebuilt to a greater width than before.

MANY of the finest suspension bridges are to be found on the American continent. John Roebling, a great American engineer, designed the Brooklyn bridge over the East river in New York. While he was preparing the designs for the bridge, his son, Washington Roebling, travelled all over Europe studying new ways of making steel wire. A year after Washington's return to America, John Roebling had his foot crushed by a boat while out surveying for the bridge. Unfortunately, he developed lock-jaw through this mishap and died in July 1869. Washington was appointed to succeed his father as engineer in charge of building the bridge, and the work continued.

Caissons had to be sunk and driven deep into the river bed for the foundations of the piers. On the Brooklyn side of the river the caisson was sunk to 44 feet below high water, but on the New York side it proved necessary to sink the caisson 78 feet.

The caissons, which were made mainly of timber, had walls 9 feet thick. The roof of the Brooklyn caisson was 15 feet thick, while that of the New York one was 22 feet thick, for it had to sink deeper and withstand greater pressures. When the caissons were built, they were floated out and sunk in their positions by building stonework on top of them until they sank to the river bed. Compressed air pipes were then connected up to them and work started.

During work on the Brooklyn caisson, a fire started in the roof and was driven deep into the woodwork by the compressed air. To put the fire out the whole caisson finally had to be flooded. During the fighting of this fire, Washington Roebling had spent many hours under compressed air directing operations. In fact he spent more hours under these conditions than any other man working on the bridge. Eventually this had its effect on his health and he remained crippled and partly paralysed for the rest of his life.

When the stone towers of the bridge were completed, four huge steel cables were spun over the tops of the towers from the Brooklyn to the New York

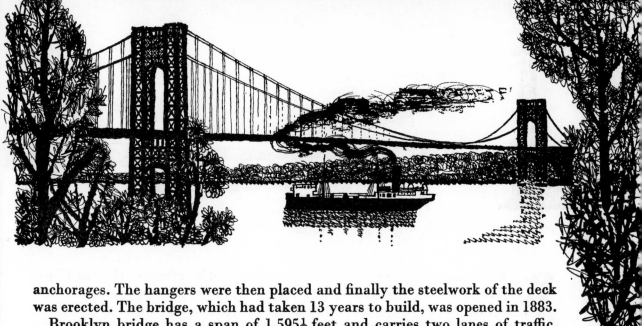

anchorages. The hangers were then placed and finally the steelwork of the deck was erected. The bridge, which had taken 13 years to build, was opened in 1883.

Brooklyn bridge has a span of 1,595½ feet and carries two lanes of traffic, two elevated railway tracks, two lines for street cars and a footway.

Following the success of Brooklyn bridge, two more cable suspension bridges were built in New York. These were the Williamsburg bridge completed in 1903 and the Manhattan bridge in 1909. Both these bridges were suspended from four main cables spun in position in the same way as those on the Brooklyn bridge.

The George Washington bridge, over the mighty Hudson river, was designed to carry two decks, one above the other. Only the upper deck has so far been built. This deck carries eight lanes of traffic. Four more lanes of heavy traffic will be carried by this bridge when the lower deck is built.

The deck of the George Washington bridge is suspended from four giant steel-wire cables each three feet thick and built up from 26,474 wires. If all the wires used in these cables were laid end to end, they would stretch for 105,000 miles. That is about four times round the world. These four cables are together capable of holding up a weight of 90,000 tons, and their ends are buried in tremendous stone anchorage blocks containing 500,000 tons of stonework.

Two steel towers 595 feet high hold the cables suspended across the river. At first it was planned to encase these towers in concrete and face them with granite. This, however, has not been carried out.

When the cable-spinning was finished and the hangers had been fixed, two travelling cranes, working from the towers towards the centre of the bridge, built out the deck in front of themselves, laying it section by section.

The span of the George Washington bridge is 3,500 feet and the deck is suspended 150 feet above the high-water level of the river. Despite its great size the building of the bridge was completed in only four years. The total cost was 75 million dollars. It is said to carry as many as 5 million vehicles in a year.

17

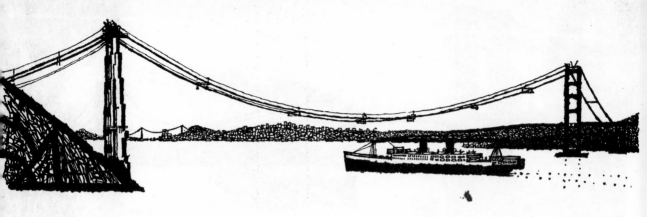

WHEN ships sail out of San Francisco Bay in the evening, they sail into the golden rays of the setting sun. Because of this the strait through which they sail to reach the Pacific Ocean is known as the 'Golden Gate'. Over this strait now stands the great Golden Gate bridge. This slender and graceful bridge has a span of 4,200 feet and carries a 90-foot wide deck suspended from two cables, each three feet thick.

This is no ordinary bridge over a river and it presented the designers with many new problems. The piers had to be built deep down on the bed of the ocean. The north pier was founded 20 feet and the south pier 100 feet below water. Divers had to be sent down to work on the foundations, and because of the speed at which the water rushes through the narrow strait when tides are changing, they could only work for very short periods at the turn of the tides. The north pier was built inside a timber frame weighed down with broken rock and surrounded with sheet steel. The south pier was constructed inside a huge fender. The men who worked on the bridge nicknamed the fender the 'bathtub', and that nickname describes it well. It was 300 feet long and 155 feet wide, and was set on rock on the ocean bed. The rock had to be dug away and levelled where the fender was to be placed. This work was carried out in an unusual way. Small holes were drilled in the rock and into these small explosive bombs were placed. The bombs were exploded making larger holes in the rock. Into the enlarged holes larger bombs were placed. These were all exploded at once breaking the rock up into sections which could be dredged out.

Since the 'bathtub' was 1,125 feet out from the shore, a long jetty was built out to it on wooden piles driven into the bed of the ocean. Soon after the jetty had been built, a steamer ran into it in a thick fog and carried away a 300-foot section of it. When this section had been rebuilt, a violent storm broke out and this time 800 feet of the jetty broke away. However, this section was rebuilt and work soon started on the 'bathtub'.

The 'bathtub' itself was made by pouring concrete under water into steel box shutters, and was gradually built up in this way until all but one side was well

18

above high-water level. It was planned to float a giant caisson weighing 8,000 tons into the 'bathtub' through the side that had been left open. The caisson was floated in successfully, but once inside, it was bounced about so much by the sea that it was in danger of smashing down the walls of the 'bathtub'. The engineers decided that they must give up all ideas of sinking the caisson as they had planned, so it was towed out of the 'bathtub' and was finally taken far out into the Pacific Ocean and sunk.

It was then decided to build the south pier in the 'bathtub' itself. The side that had been left below water was built up to the same level as the other sides and 29 feet of concrete added to the 36 feet already in the bottom of it. The water in the 'bathtub' was then pumped out, and the building of the south pier was commenced on the concrete base.

Two steel towers were built up from the piers, each rising to a height of 746 feet. They were built section after section by electrically operated derricks which were hauled up as they completed each stage of the building. The cables were spun over the tops of the towers, and anchored at their ends. The deck was built out from either end and suspended by hangers from the two main cables. The Golden Gate bridge was opened in May 1937.

Construction of the deep south pier of the Golden Gate Bridge

THE only bridge outside the American continent to be built with the same parallel wire construction as has been used on many American bridges, is the Otto Beit bridge over the Zambezi river in Rhodesia.

This suspension bridge has a main span of 1,050 feet, and its total length is 1,210 feet. It carries a roadway 34½ feet wide, and is part of a scheme to improve roadways in South Africa. The Otto Beit bridge is designed to carry a moving load of 16 tons. The steelwork and cables of this bridge weigh a total of 1,242 tons.

Between the great North American lakes of Michigan and Huron lie the Straits of Mackinac. Across these straits now stands the mighty Mackinac bridge. This bridge was built to link the cities of St. Ignace, on the northern, and Mackinaw on the southern peninsula of the state of Michigan. The bridge, which was opened in November 1957, carries four lanes of traffic across the straits.

The whole distance from St. Ignace to Mackinaw is just over 5 miles, and the bridge itself covers nearly 3½ miles. The main span, which is 3,800 feet, is in the form of a suspension bridge, while the approaches to the span are of girder construction. The 33 under-water piers are constructed of concrete, two of these being for the main towers, two for the anchorages and the rest to support the girder approaches. The concrete for the piers was poured in by a fleet of self-pouring vessels, each carrying about 10,000 tons of concrete and capable of discharging its load at a rate of 2,500 tons in an hour. The foundations of the piers alone took 440,000 cubic yards of concrete to build, and cost 25,735,000 dollars. Some of them had to be sunk to as much as 206 feet below the surface of the water.

Since the suspension part of the Mackinac bridge is near the centre of the straits, the anchorages for the main cables had to be built into huge anchorage piers, and not ashore.

The two main towers, which support the main suspension cables, are made of steel and stand 552 feet above the water. The steel used in the construction of the towers weighed a total of 13,000 tons, and they cost 7,250,000 dollars to build. So that inspection of the insides of the towers can be carried out easily, a lift was installed in one leg of each of them.

The climate in the part of America where the Mackinac bridge stands brought problems of its own to both the designers and the builders of the bridge, for the winters are so severe that the waters of the lakes turn to ice, which may become very thick. In the winter of 1954-55, when engineers made an examination of the ice in the Straits of Mackinac, they found it to be 18 inches thick, but that was during a fairly mild winter. Ice can exert tremendous pressures and these were allowed for in the design of the bridge piers, which were built to withstand ice pressures of 115,000 pounds for every foot around the piers.

On a structure as large as the Mackinac bridge, wind can also exert tremendous pressures, and winds of up to 100 miles per hour had to be allowed for.

The Mackinac bridge, which was estimated to cost over 80,000,000 dollars, is expected to have paid for itself by the year 1975. The bridge will earn money from the tolls paid by people crossing it. The tolls will be collected in six toll-booths where cars will drive in before crossing the bridge. It will be possible for as many as 1,500 vehicles per hour to cross on each of the traffic lanes.

Not all the bridges that have been built have been successful. In 1830, the first railway suspension bridge was built to carry the Stockton and Darlington railway over the river Tees. This bridge was unsatisfactory from the start, for the deck sagged under the weight of trains passing over it, and rose in a huge wave in front of them. After only a few years in use, the bridge was torn to pieces by all this bending.

In 1940, the Tacoma Narrows bridge was built in the United States of America. This suspension bridge was the third longest in the world. It was an extremely beautiful bridge, slender and graceful, but very soon after it was opened it earned for itself the nickname of 'Galloping-Gertie'. This unfortunate name was given to the bridge because of its peculiar behaviour in the wind. Even in quite light winds the deck of the bridge would start to sway and waves would run along it as though some giant hand were shaking it. The waves in the deck were sometimes so high that people driving cars over it found the cars ahead of them disappearing from view behind the waves. All suspension bridges sway a little in the wind, but this one had tricks of its own. Apart from the swaying and waving, the deck would tip over at an angle, first one way and then the other. Many attempts were made to stop these movements of the deck, but they all failed and, only four months after the bridge had been completed, the deck collapsed in a wind of only 42 miles per hour, although the bridge had been designed to withstand winds of 120 miles per hour. The bridge has since been rebuilt with stiffening trusses under the deck to prevent the movements that broke it up before.

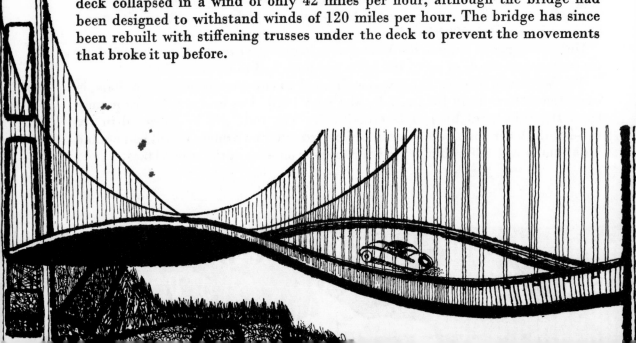

Probably the best known and, at the same time, the most terrible of bridge disasters was that which befell the old Tay bridge. This bridge, designed by Sir Thomas Bouch, was completed in 1878 and was hailed as a great engineering achievement. It was, at the time, the longest bridge over water in the world. It was a girder bridge, built in a series of spans over 2 miles of the Firth of Tay in Scotland. To allow shipping to pass underneath it, the 13 largest spans were situated in the middle of the bridge. These covered half a mile, and were set on cast iron columns on brick and concrete piers. The bridge was built to carry a single track railway on the line from Edinburgh to Aberdeen.

On the 28th of December 1878 a storm blew up and the wind howled along the Firth of Tay. By evening the storm had reached such violence that some local people began to wonder if the bridge would stand up to the force of such a wind. A few people went to the northern signal box to watch the bridge. By about a quarter past seven, when the storm had built up to its full fury, the mail train started to move out across the bridge. Slowly the train moved out over the waters of the Firth, gradually disappearing into the darkness. The watchers strained their eyes after it. Suddenly they saw a flash out in the darkness and a streamer of light fell and vanished into the dark waters. The signalman then found that the telegraph lines were dead. Two men crawled out in the darkness to find part of the bridge gone. The whole train, with 75 people aboard, together with half a mile of the bridge, had disappeared beneath the waters of the Firth of Tay.

The new Tay bridge was built alongside the foundations of the old one. This bridge, which was opened in 1887, is 2 miles 73 yards long and carries two railway tracks over 85 spans, 77 feet above the Tay waters.

At the time of the Tay bridge disaster, plans had been prepared for a suspension bridge to be built over the Firth of Forth : in fact work had actually been started on the bridge. The failure of the Tay bridge had put such fears into people's minds concerning the effect of wind on bridge structures, and so little was really known about it, that the plans for the suspension bridge were put aside. Sir John Fowler and Sir Benjamin Baker were appointed to design a bridge strong enough to stand up to the winds in such an exposed position. Together they designed a bridge of steel to be built on the cantilever principle. Cantilever is only another name for a bracket. The Sydney Harbour bridge, mentioned earlier in this book, was built on this principle. Two giant brackets were built out from either side until they met in the middle.

The Forth bridge consists of three great double cantilevers, the centres of which were built as four-legged towers, each 361 feet high. The towers were made from steel tubes, some large enough to drive a London tube-train through. These tremendous tubes were built up from curved steel plates riveted together. The foundations for the towers were set, one near either shore, and one in the middle of the Firth of Forth, on Inchgervie Island.

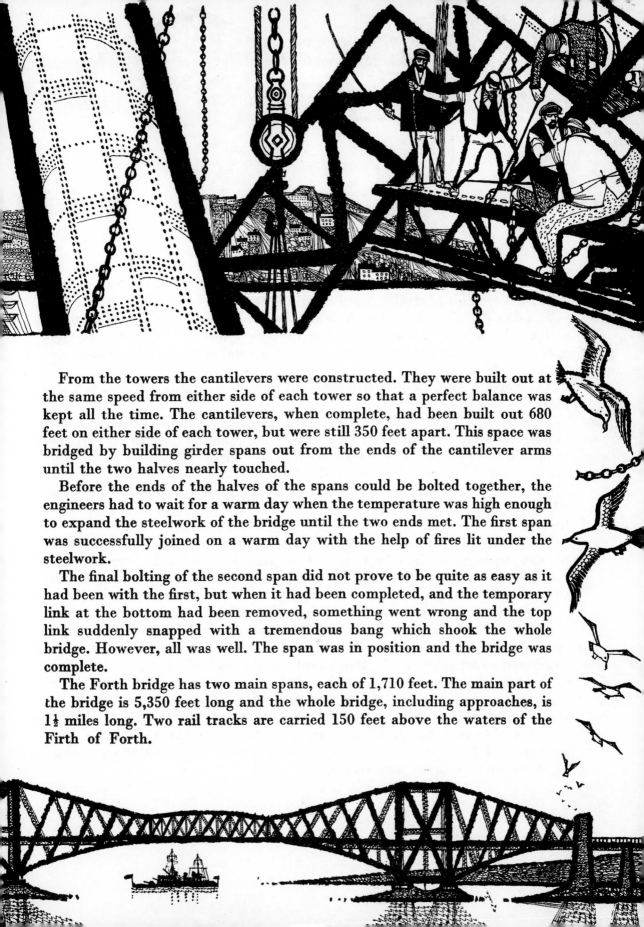

From the towers the cantilevers were constructed. They were built out at the same speed from either side of each tower so that a perfect balance was kept all the time. The cantilevers, when complete, had been built out 680 feet on either side of each tower, but were still 350 feet apart. This space was bridged by building girder spans out from the ends of the cantilever arms until the two halves nearly touched.

Before the ends of the halves of the spans could be bolted together, the engineers had to wait for a warm day when the temperature was high enough to expand the steelwork of the bridge until the two ends met. The first span was successfully joined on a warm day with the help of fires lit under the steelwork.

The final bolting of the second span did not prove to be quite as easy as it had been with the first, but when it had been completed, and the temporary link at the bottom had been removed, something went wrong and the top link suddenly snapped with a tremendous bang which shook the whole bridge. However, all was well. The span was in position and the bridge was complete.

The Forth bridge has two main spans, each of 1,710 feet. The main part of the bridge is 5,350 feet long and the whole bridge, including approaches, is 1½ miles long. Two rail tracks are carried 150 feet above the waters of the Firth of Forth.

THE steelwork of the bridge weighs a total of 50,000 tons, and to keep this vast amount of steel in good condition it has to be regularly painted. It takes the men who paint the Forth bridge three years to work from one end to the other, so that as soon as they have finished, it is time to start again. This is really not so surprising since the total area of steel to be painted works out to 145 acres.

The Forth bridge, despite 60 years and more of continual service, can still carry trains with safety at express speeds.

With the success of the Forth bridge and the failure of the Tay bridge in their minds, engineers were inclined, for a good many years, to stick to the safety of rigid bridge structures. The construction of the Forth bridge was followed by the Queensboro bridge. This bridge was built over the East river in New York City, and has two spans of 1,182 feet with a central anchor span of 630 feet on Blackwell Island. Both road and rail traffic are carried on this double-decked bridge.

The next great cantilever bridge to be built was the Quebec bridge over the St. Lawrence river in Canada. Designed to carry two rail tracks over a span of 1,800 feet, this bridge was built as two huge cantilever arms with a central suspended span between them 640 feet long.

Work on the Quebec bridge was started in 1904. The cantilever arms were built out from either side of the river and by August in 1907 the central suspended span was being built out from the ends of the arms, in the same way as the suspended girder spans on the Forth bridge had been built. It was at this stage in the building that someone noticed that some of the steel supports of the south bank cantilever were beginning to buckle. This was reported but the work continued, and the arms were built out still farther. On the morning of the 29th of August the south bank cantilever arm gave way and 9,000 tons of steel crashed down, carrying with it the 86 men who were working on it. Only 11 of these men escaped with their lives.

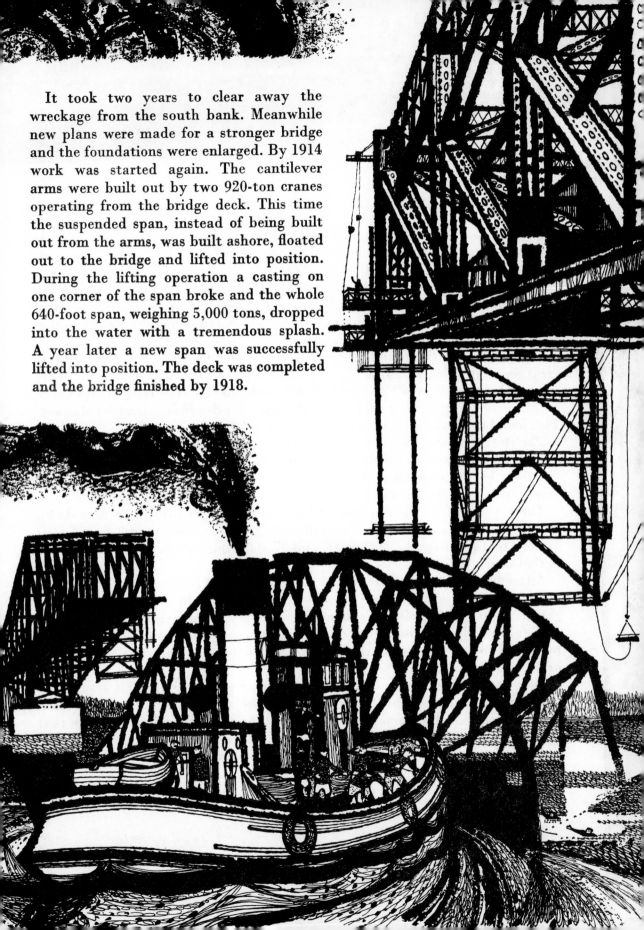

It took two years to clear away the wreckage from the south bank. Meanwhile new plans were made for a stronger bridge and the foundations were enlarged. By 1914 work was started again. The cantilever arms were built out by two 920-ton cranes operating from the bridge deck. This time the suspended span, instead of being built out from the arms, was built ashore, floated out to the bridge and lifted into position. During the lifting operation a casting on one corner of the span broke and the whole 640-foot span, weighing 5,000 tons, dropped into the water with a tremendous splash. A year later a new span was successfully lifted into position. The deck was completed and the bridge finished by 1918.

THE New Howrah bridge, opened in 1943, over the Hooghly river at Calcutta, is the third longest cantilever bridge in the world. It cost £2,500,000 to build and spans 1,500 feet.

The reinforced concrete slabs forming the foundations for the two main piers were built above ground. The slabs measured 180 feet by 81 feet on top and were built with square holes through them. The earth below the slabs was dug out and passed up and out through the holes. As the earth was removed from underneath them the foundations sank lower and lower. When one of these great concrete slabs, weighing 40,000 tons, was 90 feet below ground, it suddenly slipped through some soft ground and dropped two feet. The tremendous shock of this made the ground tremble so much that a nearby Indian temple collapsed. This foundation was finally set at a depth of 103 feet.

The steelwork was built out over the river as two huge cantilever arms. Two creeper cranes, working on the tops of the two halves of the bridge, built them out from both shores until they met in the middle of the river. The creeper cranes weighed 610 tons each.

Three years after the opening of the New Howrah bridge, in May 1946, passengers were counted over a period of 24 hours, and it was found that 121,000 foot passengers, 2,997 cattle and 27,400 vehicles passed over the bridge in that time.

Although the first concrete bridge was built by the Romans, it is really only in the last 40 or so years that reinforced concrete has been used to any great extent in bridge building. To many people's eyes these bridges, with their graceful and slender simplicity of design, are among the most beautiful ever built, and to find the best of these we have to go to either France, Switzerland, or Sweden.

Most concrete arches are built over timber or steel staging. This staging, or centering, is removed when the concrete of the arch has set. The concrete is poured over a steel framework designed to take the strains in the bridge that would otherwise break concrete on its own. When the concrete sets with the steel reinforcing inside it, the result is stronger than either concrete or steel would be on its own.

Robert Maillart, a Swiss engineer, has designed many beautiful bridges in

reinforced concrete. His Tavanasa bridge, a road bridge over the River Rhine in Switzerland, had a span of 167 feet. This lovely bridge was destroyed by a landslide in 1927.

The Salgina bridge, another of Maillart's designs, spans 295 feet across a gorge at Grisons in Switzerland. The concrete arch of this bridge is only 8 inches thick at the crown, which shows how tremendously strong reinforced concrete is, and how little material need be used to give sufficient strength provided the design is good.

Another example of Maillart's use of slender arches made from reinforced concrete can be seen in the graceful Schwandbach bridge, built over a deep ravine near Schwarzenburg. This bridge, built curved, as part of a sharp bend in the road, has a span of 111 feet, yet the arch which supports it is less than 8 inches thick throughout its entire length. It could almost be called a reinforced concrete ribbon.

The Sando bridge over the Angerman river in Sweden, with its span of 866 feet, was a tremendous achievement in reinforced concrete. It was built over a timber staging without any support from the river bed. When the concrete for the arch was being poured, the weight proved to be too much for the unsupported staging, and it collapsed. Luckily there was nobody on it at the time. The staging was rebuilt, but with supports from the river bed, and this time the concrete was successfully poured and set. The Sando bridge, which is part of a long viaduct carrying four lanes of traffic and two footpaths, was finally opened in 1943.

During the Second World War the Plougastel bridge, over the river Elorn in France, had to be put out of action. This was done by destroying the northern arch of this triple-arched bridge. When the war was over, engineers set about the task of rebuilding the northern arch. A centering was built on the shore of the river. It was constructed partly of timber and partly of concrete. When completed, the centering was floated out, on two reinforced concrete pontoons, to a position below the point where the arch was to be constructed. The

centering was then lifted off the pontoons and into position by lifting gear built on the remaining stubs of the old arch. The new arch was then poured in on the centering, which was removed after the concrete had set.

London has one very lovely reinforced concrete bridge spanning the river Thames. This is the new Waterloo bridge, which was built to replace John Rennie's Waterloo bridge built in 1817.

The new bridge carries six lanes of traffic over the Thames.

Although the new Waterloo bridge appears to be composed of five concrete arch spans, in reality it is not, for the central span was built as two cantilever arms while the other four were built as girder spans. The reinforced concrete arches that we see are only facings on either side of the bridge to give it its smooth and graceful appearance. This deception can be forgiven when we remember how well it does its job of carrying heavy traffic and at the same time lending grace and beauty to London's river scene.

We have taken a brief look at some of the world's bridges. We have seen how some have failed and how others have stood through the centuries. We have looked at many in this book, but we must remember that many, many more have been planned and built that have not been mentioned here, and as the years go by, bridges will be designed to span distances far greater than we have dreamed of.

Oxford University Press, Ely House, London W. 1

GLASGOW   NEW YORK   TORONTO   MELBOURNE   WELLINGTON
CAPE TOWN   SALISBURY   IBADAN   NAIROBI   DAR ES SALAAM   LUSAKA   ADDIS ABABA
BOMBAY   CALCUTTA   MADRAS   KARACHI   LAHORE   DACCA
KUALA LUMPUR   SINGAPORE   HONG KONG   TOKYO

Printed at Old Trafford, Manchester, by Jesse Broad & Co. Limited